Sharks and Dolphins

A Compare and Contrast Book

By Kevin Kurtz

This is a shark.

tiger shark

This is a dolphin.

bottlenose dolphin

In some ways they are similar.
In other ways they are different.

Sharks and dolphins live in the ocean.

bull shark

They both have torpedo-shaped bodies to cut through the water. They have fins and flippers in similar places to help them swim quickly.

spinner dolphin

Sharks and dolphins are not the same kind of animals, though.

Sharks are fish.

lemon shark

sea horse

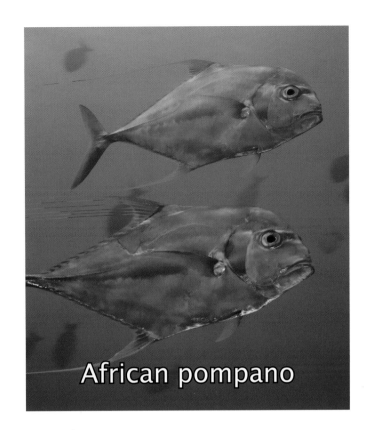

African pompano

So are these animals.

clownfish

angelfish

Dolphins are mammals.

commerson's dolphin

lion

giraffe

So are these animals.

bat

human

silky shark

Like other fish, sharks breathe underwater. They breathe with gills.

common dolphin

Like other mammals, dolphins breathe air above water. They breathe with lungs and a blowhole.

great hammerhead shark

There are over four hundred kinds of sharks.

sawfish shark

mako shark

great white shark

They all live in the ocean.

thresher shark

spiny dogfish shark

Pacific white-sided dolphin

There are thirty-eight different kinds of dolphins that live in the ocean.

bottlenose dolphin

Amazon river dolphin

There are also five kinds of dolphins that live in freshwater rivers.

The biggest sharks are whale sharks.
They can be sixty feet long.

The biggest dolphins are orcas.
They can be thirty-two feet long.

Sharks and dolphins look similar because they are both predators. They both eat fish and other animals.

blacktip reef shark

spotted dolphin

Sharks and dolphins both have sharp teeth to catch prey.

sand tiger shark

Sharks have many rows of teeth.
They are always growing new teeth.

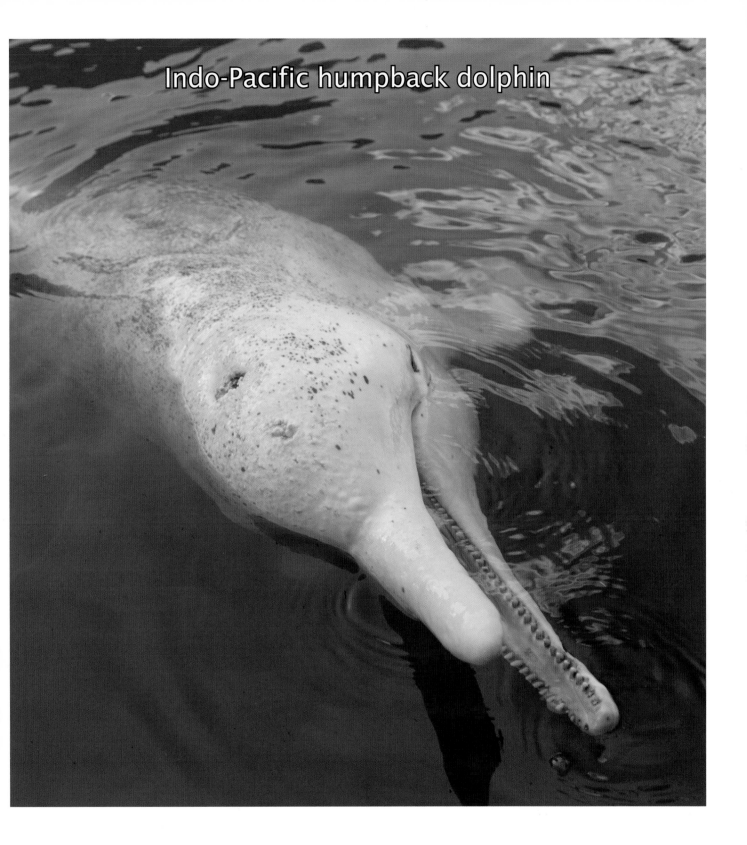

Indo-Pacific humpback dolphin

Dolphins have one row of teeth. They have the same teeth their entire lives.

whitetip reef shark

Both sharks and dolphins are important. They keep other animals from becoming overpopulated. The ocean would not be healthy without them.

bottlenose dolphin

For Creative Minds

This For Creative Minds educational section contains activities to engage children in learning while making it fun at the same time. The activities build on the underlying subjects introduced in the story. While older children may be able to do these activities on their own, we encourage adults to work with the young children in their lives. Even if the adults have long forgotten or never learned this information, they can still work through the activities and be experts in their children's eyes! Exposure to these concepts at a young age helps to build a strong foundation for easier comprehension later in life. This section may be photocopied or printed from our website by the owner of this book for educational, non-commercial uses. Cross-curricular teaching activities for use at home or in the classroom, interactive quizzes, and more are available online. Go to www.ArbordalePublishing.com and click on the book's cover to explore all the links.

Venn Diagram: Fish and Mammals

A **Venn diagram** is made of overlapping circles and shows how two things are alike and different. In the Venn diagram below, one circle shows traits belonging to fish and the other shows traits belonging to mammals. In the middle, where the circles overlap, are traits that fish and mammals have in common.

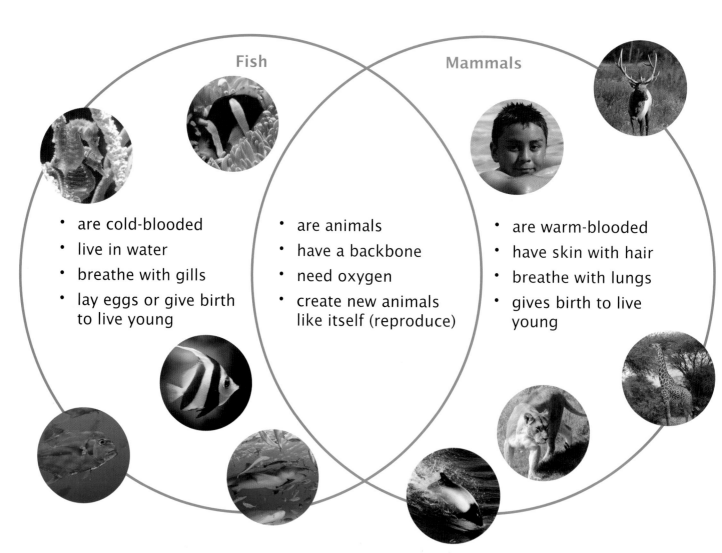

Fish

- are cold-blooded
- live in water
- breathe with gills
- lay eggs or give birth to live young

- are animals
- have a backbone
- need oxygen
- create new animals like itself (reproduce)

Mammals

- are warm-blooded
- have skin with hair
- breathe with lungs
- gives birth to live young

Draw your own Venn diagram (or print the one in the online Teaching Activity Guide) to compare sharks and dolphins.

A World Without Sharks and Dolphins

A predator is any animal that hunts other animals (prey) for food. Predators are an important part of any food web. If the top predators disappear from a food web, it affects the entire ecosystem. What could happen if sharks and dolphins were not a part of the ocean food web?

Put the following events in order to spell the scrambled word.

 Without as many small fish and algae-eaters, there would be nothing to slow the growth of algae. Algae are important to the ocean's health, but too much algae can smother coral reefs.

 Sharks and dolphins hunt mid-size ocean animals, including squid, seals, stingrays, and large fish. If sharks or dolphins disappeared, these mid-size ocean animals would have fewer predators. Their populations would grow.

 If the coral reefs and the animals they support disappeared, human fishers all around the world would not be able to catch as many fish.

 If the fishers could not catch enough fish, many people would go hungry. Three billion people (almost half of the world's population) depend on seafood as part of their diet.

 All of those mid-size ocean animals would need lots of food to eat. They would over-hunt the smaller marine life that feeds on algae, jellyfish, and plankton. The small-size ocean animals would start to disappear.

 The coral reefs smothered by algae would get sick and die. Coral reefs are an important ocean habitat. They provide shelter and food for many ocean animals. If the coral reefs died, those animals would disappear as well.

Answer: OCEANS

Sharks

Match the body part labels to their location on the shark. Answers are below.

Dorsal fins: the fins on a shark's back, used to stabilize the body in the water

Eye: the organ on the front of the face that a shark uses to see

Gills: openings on a shark's sides that allow the shark to take in oxygen from the water

Pectoral fins: the fins at a shark's sides

Pelvic fin: the small fin underneath a shark's belly

Snout: the part of a shark's face that sticks forward from the body

Tail fin: the vertical fin at the back of a shark's body

Animals use senses to learn about the world around them. Sharks have a special sense called **electroreception**. Just like many animals sense light or sound, sharks sense electricity.

When an animal moves, its muscles flex. This creates a small electric charge. Electricity travels easily through salt water.

Sharks sense the electricity in the water to find their prey.

Dolphins

Match the body part labels to their location on the dolphin. Answers are below.

Rostrum: the part of a dolphin's face that sticks forward from the body

Blowhole: opening on a dolphin's back that allow the dolphin to take in oxygen from the air

Dorsal fin: the fin on a dolphin's back, used to stabilize the body in the water

Eye: the organ on the front of the face that a dolphin uses to see

Flukes: the horizontal tail at the back of a dolphin's body

Pectoral fins: the fins at a dolphin's sides

Look at the shark body parts on the previous page. What body parts do sharks and dolphins have in common? What body parts are similar but have different names? What body parts do sharks have that dolphins don't, or vice versa?

Dolphins use **echolocation** to map their surroundings. They rely heavily on their sense of sound. Dolphins make a high-pitched squeaking noise and then listen for the echoes.

Sound moves in waves. When it hits an object, it bounces back. This is called an echo. The sound of the echo tells the dolphin what type of thing the sound bounced off. The time it takes for the echo to come back to the dolphin's ear tells it how far away the object is.

Dolphins use their sense of hearing to find their prey.

Answers: A-rostrum. B-eye. C-blowhole. D-pectoral fins. E-dorsal fin. F-flukes

Cover designed and photoshopped by Mark Lawrence.

Thanks to Shelley Dearhart, Good Catch Manager at the South Carolina Aquarium, for reviewing the accuracy of the information in this book.

Library of Congress Cataloging-in-Publication Data

Kurtz, Kevin, author.
  Sharks and dolphins : a compare and contrast book / by Kevin Kurtz.
    pages cm. -- (Compare and contrast series)
  Audience: Ages 4-8.
  Includes bibliographical references.
  ISBN 978-1-62855-732-9 (English hardcover) -- ISBN 978-1-62855-739-8 (English pbk.) -- ISBN 978-1-62855-753-4 (English downloadable ebook) -- ISBN 978-1-62855-767-1 (English interactive dual-language ebook) -- ISBN 978-1-62855-746-6 (Spanish pbk.) -- ISBN 978-1-62855-760-2 (Spanish downloadable ebook) -- ISBN 978-1-62855-774-9 (Spanish interactive dual-language ebook) 1. Sharks--Juvenile literature. 2. Dolphins--Juvenile literature. 3. Marine animals--Juvenile literature. I. Title.
  QL638.9.K87 2016
  591.77--dc23
                        2015035978

Translated into Spanish: *Tiburones y delfines*
Lexile® Level: 410
key phrases: animal classification, compare/contrast, ocean animals

Bibliography:
Cahill, Tim. Dolphins. National Geographic Books: 2000.
Connor, Richard C. The Lives of Whales and Dolphins. Henry Holt: 1994.
Parker, Steve and Jane. The Encyclopedia of Sharks. Firefly Books: 1999.

Image	Photo Source
cover	Yuri Checcucci, Thinkstock
cover	mel-nik, Thinkstock
titlepage	Olgysha, Shutterstock
tiger shark	nicolas.voisin44, Shutterstock
bottlenose dolphin	U.S. Fish and Wildlife Service
bull shark	Matt9122, Shutterstock
spinner dolphin	Shin Okamoto, Shutterstock
lemon shark	nicolas.voisin44, Shutterstock
sea horse	Lydia Jacobs, public domain
African pompano	Yann hubert, Shutterstock
clownfish	Petr Kratochvil, public domain
angelfish	Lilla Frerichs, public domain
commerson's dolphin	Rich Lindie, Shutterstock
lion	George Hodan, public domain
giraffe	Anna Langova, public domain
bat	Ivan Kuzmin, Shutterstock
human	S. Lopez, public domain
silky shark	Sergey Dubrov, Shutterstock
common dolphin	Jamen Percy, Shutterstock
great hammerhead	nicolas.voisin44, Shutterstock
sawfish shark	Petr Kratochvil, public domain
mako shark	Greg Amptman, Shutterstock
great white shark	Willyam Bradberry, Shutterstock
thresher shark	nicolas.voisin44, Shutterstock
spiny dogfish shark	Boris Pamikov, Shutterstock
Pacific white-sided dolphin	Tom Kieckhefer, NOAA
bottlenose dolphin	vkilikov, Shutterstock
amazon river dolphin	Erni, Shutterstock
whale shark	Andrea Izzotti, Shutterstock
orca	Tatiana Ivkovich, Shutterstock
blacktip reef shark	Ruth Black, Shutterstock
spotted dolphin	Willyam Bradberry, Shutterstock
sand tiger shark	Dray van Beeck, Shutterstock
Indo-Pacific humpback dolphin	momopixs, Shutterstock
whitetip reef shark	Kjersti Joergensen, Shutterstock
bottlenose dolphin	Willyam Bradberry, Shutterstock

Manufactured in China, December 2015
This product conforms to CPSIA 2008
First Printing

Arbordale Publishing
Mt. Pleasant, SC 29464
www.ArbordalePublishing.com